Mickey Maloney - Spy

Written by Jill Eggleton
Illustrated by Trevor Pye

Toronto, ON M1E 3V4

Childhood Days

Mickey Maloney was born in Swizel. He had five older sisters. Some people said Mickey Maloney was lucky to have five sisters, but Mickey thought it was very unlucky to have five sisters and even more unlucky to be the youngest.

Mickey was a very nosy baby. He learnt to crawl like a caterpillar when he was just three months old. As soon as a door was opened, Mickey Maloney would be off, crawling on his little fat tummy into the garden. He loved to be in the garden. He would pull all the leaves off the cabbages, trying to find slugs and would dig for worms in the dirt with his baby fingers.

But mostly, Mickey loved the snails. He loved to let them crawl all over his arms and legs.

Even when Mickey Maloney learnt to walk, he still would rather crawl. People used to think it was very strange. But Mickey Maloney said he saw all sorts of things when he was down low on the ground.

3

On his seventh birthday Mickey Maloney's grandfather gave him a magnifying glass. It was Mickey's favourite present and he took it everywhere with him. He took the magnifying glass to school and charged the other kids twenty cents a look. He made enough money from his magnifying glass to buy a book on secret codes.

He found out that he could see things the other kids couldn't. He said one day he saw something in another kid's hair. The teacher said he shouldn't be looking at other people's hair and made Mickey leave his magnifying glass at home after that.

Happy Birthday

Love from Grandfather xxx

Mickey Maloney made his first spy kit when he was seven years old. He made it in an old box. He was very proud of his spy kit. He decided he needed a special place to hide all his spy gear, so he cut a hole underneath his mattress and put in a zip.

Nobody knew about his secret hiding place until they moved house and carried out the mattress. Mickey had left the zip undone and all his spy gear tumbled onto the ground. Mickey Maloney's mother was mad about the hole in the mattress and Mickey Maloney was mad because he had to find another secret hiding place.

Mickey Maloney practised being a spy on his five sisters. Every week he picked one sister to spy on. He would hide in all sorts of places – behind curtains, in rubbish bins, under beds.

Mickey Maloney said he found out how much junk food his sisters ate in a week and reported that to his mother. He found out how long they spent on the telephone and reported that to his father. He found out a lot of secret things they didn't tell their parents.

Monday:
Phone call by Jill
started 3:00pm

Ended...

Mickey kept all the information about his sisters in a black notebook. One day, however, his sister caught him hiding in her closet. She was really mad and she cut up his black notebook. That was the end of Mickey Maloney's important information about his sisters.

Mickey Maloney tried spying on his parents but they weren't that easy to spy on. He did find out that his father was a chocolate thief. Even in the middle of the night he would creep around the house pinching chocolates. He reported this information to his mother but she said she already knew, so he gave up spying on them! He decided that it was only any good spying on people if you could pass on some information that nobody knew.

Mickey Maloney's favourite subject at school was science. He loved finding out how things worked. He loved reading books about spies. His favourite book was about a famous spy who spied on animals all over the world. Mickey read everything he could about this spy. He was very interested in how long his spy hero sat perched in a tree waiting for information.

Mickey Maloney practised tree-sitting too. He would spend hours up in a tree with his magnifying glass and notebook. His family got worried about his behaviour and took him to a doctor. But the doctor said that there was nothing wrong with Mickey and that "having five sisters would be enough to make anyone spend hours in a tree".

Mickey the School Leaver

When Mickey Maloney left school, he went to work at the zoo. His main job was to clean out the elephant's pen. He hated this job. He couldn't believe that elephants could drop such huge loads so often! When Mickey Maloney finished cleaning up the elephant pen, he would spy on the animals. He found out some very interesting things. He saw many animals stealing and bullying. Mickey Maloney reported this information to the zoo manager.

The zoo manager was very pleased. He promoted Mickey to Animal Protection Officer.

Mickey Maloney's new job was to look for anyone acting suspiciously around the animals and report them to the manager.

Mickey Maloney loved this job. He found people doing all sorts of things they shouldn't be. One day, he watched a woman pulling out the feathers from ostriches. Mickey Maloney discovered that this woman owned a hat shop and that her hats were famous for their ostrich feathers. Mickey Maloney reported this information to the zoo manager. The manager was very pleased and gave Mickey Maloney a pay rise.

The University Years

Mickey Maloney stayed at the zoo for two years, but his father said he wasn't using his brain just hanging about at the zoo. He thought Mickey should go to university. So Mickey Maloney went to university and studied hard.

In the holidays, Mickey worked in an ice-cream factory so he could pay for his university fees. It was a boring job but Mickey Maloney used his magnifying glass to check out the ice cream. He found all sorts of things that had slipped into the ice cream. He found a button; he found a ring; he even found a contact lens.

The manager was very pleased with Mickey Maloney because he said Mickey had saved his factory and people's jobs. If someone had swallowed a contact lens, the factory could have been put out of business.

After four years at university, Mickey graduated. He could write *Mickey Maloney* with *B.Sc* after his name. His sisters said that B.Sc stood for boy scout.

Spy School Days

Mickey Maloney looked for jobs after university, but he couldn't find anything he wanted to do. Then, one day, he saw an advertisement in the paper for Spy School. Mickey knew that he wanted to be a spy.

Spy School was tough. Mickey Maloney had to get up very early and he didn't get home until late at night. At Spy School, he learnt how to disguise himself. His favourite disguise was a green hat, orange hair and big square sunglasses.

He learnt how to creep and sneak, and how to send secret messages.

He learnt how to spot clues, and make traps.

He learnt spy words, like 'tail', 'shadow', and 'drop'.

Mickey spent three years at Spy School. At the end of that time he sat a test. A spy teacher had to spend a whole day following Mickey Maloney while he spied.

But Mickey Maloney was such a good spy, he ended up following the teacher.

Mickey Maloney B.Sc, B.Sp

Mickey Maloney graduated again but, this time, it was a secret. (No one is allowed to know when spies graduate.)

Now he could write more letters after his name – Mickey Maloney B.Sc, B.Sp. He was very pleased when Big Wig from the Spy School gave him a job on his spy team.

Mickey Maloney still works for Big Wig. He has become a very clever spy and Big Wig uses him for his most difficult jobs.

Mickey Maloney loves being a spy.
He says the job is always interesting.
He never knows what he will be
doing from one day to the next.
Mickey Maloney says he will still be
a spy when he is an old man.

Once a spy, always a spy, he says.

Biography

A **BIOGRAPHY** is a story of a person's life written by another person.

How to Write a Biography

Step 1

Choose a person that you want to write about.

Think of some questions you want to ask the person.

QUESTIONS TO ASK:

Where were you born?

What things can you tell us about your family?

Where did you live?

Where did you go to school?

What interesting things have happened to you?

What are your likes and dislikes?

Step 2

Interview the person and make notes.

MICKEY MALONEY —

Born in Swizel. / Had five sisters.

Thought he was unlucky to be the youngest.

Look at your notes and make a plan.

Childhood Days After the School Years

 University Spy School Days

Step 4 Use your plan to write the biography.

Step 5 Check your biography.

Can you add anything to make it more interesting?

Can you use timelines, sketches, photographs...?

Have you left anything out?

Can you take anything out that is not important?

Remember...

If the biography is about a person who lived long ago or in a far-off place, use your library or the Internet to find out information about them. Then you can use the same steps to write up their biography.

Guide Notes

Title: Mickey Maloney – Spy
Stage: Fluency

Text Form: Biography
Approach: Guided Reading
Processes: Thinking Critically, Exploring Language, Processing Information
Written and Visual Focus: Book Layout

THINKING CRITICALLY
(sample questions)
- Why do you think Mickey Maloney was an interesting character to write about?
- What sort of things could you say about Mickey Maloney's character?
- What do you think are the most interesting things about his life?
- If this biography was to continue, what do you think the next chapter of his life would be about?

EXPLORING LANGUAGE

Terminology
Spread, author, illustrator, credits, imprint information, ISBN number

Vocabulary
Clarify: magnifying, reported, subject, perched, bullying, protection, promoted, suspiciously, graduated
Adjectives: *junk* food, *boring* job, *green* hat, *orange* hair, *clever* spy, *nosy* baby
Homonyms: hole/whole, week/weak, there/their, four/for
Antonyms: lucky/unlucky, end/begin, clean/unclean, saved/lost
Synonyms: best/favourite, manager/boss, job/occupation
Abbreviation: B.Sc (Bachelor of Science)
Simile: crawl like a caterpillar

Print Conventions
Apostrophes – possessive (people's hair), contraction (can't)
Dash: Mickey Maloney – Spy
Inverted commas – 'tail', 'shadow'